Lonesome times when no one's there,

plants are there for you.

Very unique and special,

they come in many colors too.

Oxygen we need,

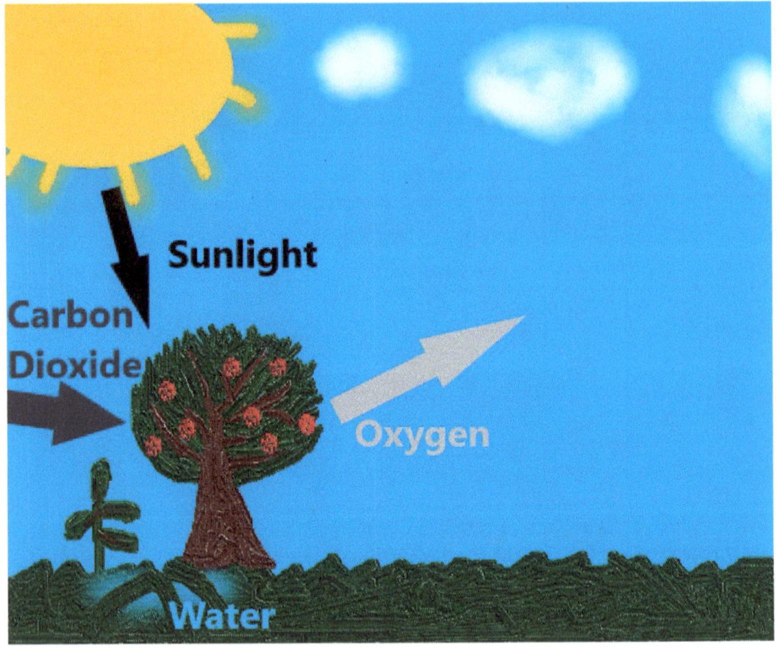

without plants we can't make it through.

Everlasting happiness,

they bring along with their presence too.

The living thing that says no words,

just bends.

Has no power,

based from what we commend.

Extreme cruelty we give to them,

that has got to end.

Popping out with joy,

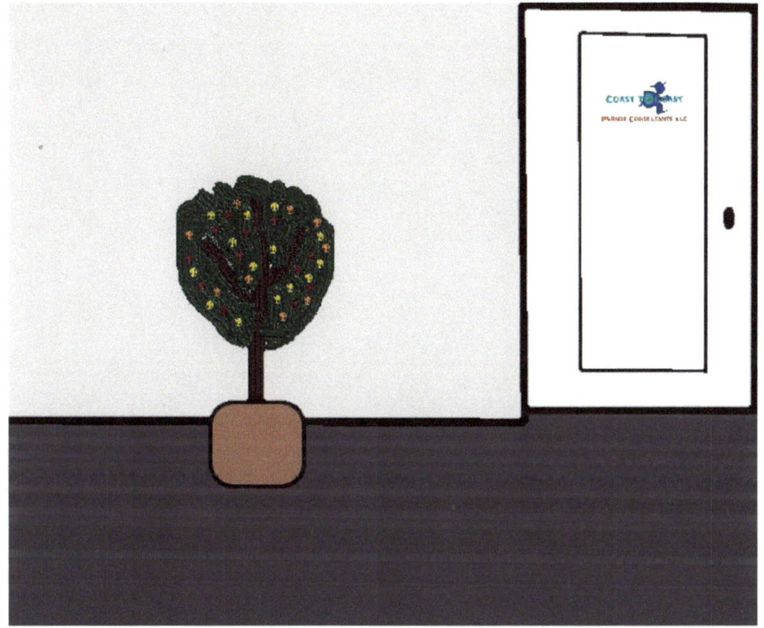

plants arouse any room.

Leaving the dark behind,

and bring a spark as they gloom.

Another reason why being cruel will bring us doom.

Now it's time to act, not ignore the elephant in the room.

Time to love the plant,

don't be cruel and watch them bloom.

How can little seeds grow into a gigantic lovely tree?

Once seeds are planted with proper fertilization,

All they need are water and sunlight.

Then they begin to sprout.

Once they sprout out the ground,

We begin to witness life of a baby plant.

Growing every single day and night,

The little plant transforms into a young adult.

While providing the entire world with oxygen,

Plants turn out to become one of the most
beautiful living things in the world.

Let's love the plants,

They need us just like we need them.

The End.